Like Lions!

selected poems of Julian Tuwim
translated by Patrick Wang

Like Lions!

My deepest gratitude to Ms. Ewa Tuwim-Wozniak and the Fundacja im. Juliana Tuwima i Ireny Tuwim for permission to publish these poems. I am also deeply indebted to Ms. Kasia Kietlinska for her careful review and insightful feedback on early drafts of these poems.

All poems by Julian Tuwim © Copyright by Fundacja im. Juliana Tuwima i Ireny Tuwim, Warsaw 2006, Poland

English translations © Copyright 2023 by Patrick Wang
All rights reserved.

First Edition
ISBN: 978-1-7356865-8-5

Contents

from *Lurking Round God* (1918)

Theophany	3
Soul	4
Fire	5
Fortune	6
Painter	7
Covenant	8
A Song of Rapture and Rhythm	9
Succession	10
Pan	11
Helios	12
Christ	13
Birthday Child	14
City Christ	15
The Elderly	17
Hospital Gardens	18
Symphony of Ages	19
Attack	20
How Verse Arises	21
Peaches	22
Betrayal	23
Lily	24

from *Socrates Dancing* (1920)
  Our Wisdom   27
  Vanitas   28
  Dialogue   29
  Worn Down by Frenzied Tempests…   30
  Litany   31
  Beggars' Frost   33
  Socrates Dancing   35
  Two Winds   39
  My Life   40

from *The Seventh Autumn* (1922)
  Name   43
  Angry Poem   44
  Fatherland   45

from *The Fourth Volume of Poems* (1923)
  Death   49
  We—People   50
  Instruction   51
  Reckoning   53
  In the Forest   55
  Slaughtered Birches   56

from *Words in Blood* (1926)

    Word and Flesh   59

    Rush   64

    Let Words Draw Blood!   65

    Boots   66

    The Apartment   67

    Cocktail   68

    Report on the Trip to the Exhibition...   69

    Fantastic Stroll through the Forest...   70

    Back Then   71

    Unknown Tree   72

from *The Czarnolas Matter* (1929)

    The Source   77

    Mathematics   78

    Bagdad, *or About a Future* Poet   79

    Melody   80

    About My Table   81

    A Word About the Moon in the Pond   82

    Ceiling   83

from *The Gypsy Bible* (1933)

    The Gypsy Bible   87

Grass	88
Sum of Autumn	89
Muse	90
Maytime Toil	91
To the Common Man	92

from *The Burning Essence* (1936)

Forty Springs	97
The Blizzard	98
And So It Was…	99
Distant Tiger	101
Early Spring	103
Empty Apartment	104
***With the last crumbs of youth…	105
Erratum	106
To God	107

Other Poems (1911-1943)

The Child Before the Toy Store	111
Request	112
Poem	113
Warsaw	114
The Harvest	115
Father	116

from

Lurking Round God
1918

THEOPHANY

Coming! How I foresee Thee! As a distant glowing
Of lightning reddening its massive potency!
Seeing you, sacred dream of golden bowstrings!
Seeing you—sunrise dawning—coming, o New Poetry!

Though your countenance I still have not distinguished,
From which God springs the secret essence of the ages,
Surely, you'll be maddening, you'll be mysterious,
O Soul that's coming as that dawn advances!

Your name will terrify, creatively, "I am so!"
You'll manage everything yourself, tyrannic, monstrous!
Revealing to the world—a Fiery Manifesto:
—I've come for all the madmen's dreams, rebellious abbess!

SOUL

"Apocalypse is borne within each beastly creature."
—Słowacki

It shows itself. And instinct that is sudden and secret
Recollects itself. Like thunderstorms bellowing!
Terrible truth whips in the face—or shining spirit
Permeates me: and deceives, deludes while poisoning…

Or slings itself—and pierces with its edges sharpened
My most sensitive nerve—and startles my whole being!
Or else it comes to me when I am in the garden,
Satisfying sight of golden sun retreating.

It's all around: in bygone gods who came before us,
And in that hazy hinting, in the maybe notion,
And in blind thickets of the proud and ancient forests,
And in the ghosts who throw star sobbing in the ocean.

And in those who are dying in the midday sun,
And in those who are cursing, in those who are blessing.
In those who Christs deceive, the kissing charlatans,
And in those who beneath the crosses rollick leching.

Everywhere! Troubling, pleasing, dreams of doubt releasing,
Covertly from behind, it pulverizes, tempers,
Calms and terrifies, in universewide gleaming!
—Apocalypse is borne within each beastly creature.

FIRE

O be to me, life of art, a block of many faces,
Mercilessly icy in its symmetry,
That you'd be hardness, pureness, never change your basis
And form a comprehensive mystic harmony.

And be to me diamantine. So when the sun of heaven
Passes through caressing you with golden lighting,
Blindingly you'll glisten, flashing oscillations,
A million sparks at play, ignited into shining!

Because you know, o artful life, o curious diamond,
Once cut in act of harmony with purest knowledge,
That you were borne in starry surges by the ocean,
So I could catch you—scarred upon the fiery forehead.

FORTUNE

The world has lost its wonder,
Its splendid urban scenes:
They've nothing left to utter,
Mute like roadside weeds.

Who needs all these humans,
To scrutinize in throngs:
I am fine with just one,
Whoever comes along.

Nor do books excite me
—Scoff at me if you wish—
Without books I still know plenty
For I know what it is to exist.

Beneath a tree I sojourn,
Calm and all alone—
O God! O my good fortune!
My gratitude explodes!

PAINTER

To sun, that at my window shoots a golden beacon,
In pollened millions, in a sideways streaming sliver,
I exhale with Rafael's creative bedlam,
Puffs of smoke, the cigarette's own clouds of silver.
And in the sky-blue heaven, resembling stacks of snow,
White clouds poke out, projecting out into the open
Migratory dreams of suns that know no coast,
Forever sinking into lush, susurrant oceans.

COVENANT

Submersion, soul, submersion
Through silver releasing the pigeons
With olive branches thriving.

The pigeon wings evolving,
With joyful news revolving,
Returning with curious tidings.

That God for us breeds orchards,
Bright God—a House he offers
Measured with dancing steps.

At God the sun is smiling
Beyond the House is shining
Our rainbow Covenant.

A SONG OF RAPTURE AND RHYTHM

The stars aglow in heaven.

In space—a billion universes.

Calmness.

I rest my forehead in my palm and *think*.

Not dream.

Awoke in me a great Reality,
Truth, that's flung into the eyes,
Truth that is, visibly, solely,
Eternal:

I—beneath this massive stellar cupola,
I—whose mind its aggregate is gripping,
I saturate with it, I melt myself with it.
Slowly—within me—I meet with myself:
With wondrous rapture and wondrous rhythm.

All I was thinking and speaking and doing,
Was merely this investigation
Into the all-embracing:
Whereafter within me I rest in rapture,
Tucked inside a copious calmness,
And when my heartbeat rhythm matches everything
That surrounds me.
Enough. The words are needless.

SUCCESSION

Plunged into endless existence, into a turnstile of puzzles,
I'm summoned at the pleasure of the proud Creator
To battle a mystery: succession through ages of struggles,
Although I know this is a fight I shall not weather.

I'm scrambling, successor to a blasphemous battle,
I see my bloody fight is vacuous and pointless.
I fight—and eye the end, where everything's dismantled,
I, some link within the chain of Pious Purpose.

And when my end of days I finally encounter
And see I have not taken one step forward, only
I'll pass the battle to another, who too will founder,
Deceived by the immensity of patrimony.

PAN

Pan, saucy sylvan satyr, Greco-Slavic creature,
Insane divinity of spring with Polish penchant,
A madcap-monarch, radiant, a pagan preacher,
I snort, I am in stitches, drunk in celebration!

Who wouldn't laugh?! I lay in woods as dawn draws nearer,
My hoof beats on the pine trunk... Over me—the songbirds
And sun... So well I laugh, sublime god-creature,
Until the wild and sprawling backwoods bushes shudder.

I lay, ingenious goat... And I'll get up, I'll skitter,
I'll huff, I'll knock, I'll rumble, frightening the squirrel,
I'll drag into the junipers from out the river
That Krista with the copper hair, the miller's girl!

HELIOS

On the street at its faraway edges
There the golden-cheeked sunrise he blushes!
   He is blushing so, he is flushing so,
     Hollo, glory! Radiating so!

Roseating the translucent distance,
Escalating his fiery presence!
   He is rising up, he is rolling out,
     Hollo, glory! Magnifying now!

And the tongues of the sun's inflammation
Titillating the gravelly pavement!
   He is kissing them and caressing them!
     Hollo, glory! Venerating them!

CHRIST

I don't complain, my Master, I don't complain, my Father,
That thou delivered unto my heart this love so somber.

I don't complain, my Father, how desolate my journey,
That on this thorny pathway I've grown so very weary.

Good news passed through the cabins: "It comes, by grace of heaven."
And people say: "Godspeed…" And a slice of bread is given.

So are my words that hopelessly difficult to fathom?
They do not see that it is now come: Your Sacred Kingdom.

They do not see that heaven has opened to all nations,
They don't believe although I expound with joy and patience.

But, Lord, I don't complain that my journey's so distressing,
Or that my thorny path doesn't have… it has no ending.

Small birds they have their nests, and the foxes have their stashes,
And yet the Son of Man he has nowhere he relaxes.

But Lord, I'm not complaining… Just grant this modest marvel,
That they might understand me these kindly, quiet people.

BIRTHDAY CHILD

You the foreigners within this massive city,
Who also have no home nor kin in some obscure place,
You who live in lonely emptiness and misery,
And possibly today you celebrate your birthday.

You who sit on winter evenings at the table,
Gazing in cold corners of unfriendly lodgings,
In frock coat faded gray and eaten through with moth holes,
Or in a dressing gown that's comically stodgy.

The gray indifference of hours is an outrage
That wounds you in your heartfelt ceremony;
That there is no one here to wish you happy birthday,
Unhappy birthday child, anonymous and lonely.

You who have no place to redirect your paces
When mildew of gray boredom overgrows your dwellings.
O my unhappy ones! Please cease with all your anguish!
They come your way today: the City Christ's bright greetings!

CITY CHRIST

They danced over bridges,
They danced all the evening.

Rejects, thugs, executioners,
Hangers-on and hookers,
Siphillytics, killers,
Rascals, robbers, vodka terrors.

They danced over bridges,
They danced until morning.

Trollops and mendicants,
Lunatics, shifty snoopers,
Dancing street dances,
Guillotines and streetlamps,
Swoopers.

They danced over bridges
Guests distinguished:
Miscreants!

Old lecherous men, procurers,
Bashful masturbators.
Grabbing hands with others,
Feet begin their stomping,
Sound harmonies, harmonics,
Sound until dawning,
Dancing their dance barbaric:
Further! Further!
Gorging. Drinking. Dancing.

And there was one stranger,
There was one unfamiliar,
They looked upon him scowling,
Shoulders shrugging,
Spitting.

They took him aside:
Prattling, prattling, asking,
Silence.

Rusty approached him, reddened:
—Who are you then?
  Silence.

A second approached him, nose missing,
Blotchy-skinned:
—Who are you then?
  Silence.

A drunk approached him, drawling:
—Who are you then?
  Silence.

Magdalene approached him:
She recognized, she cried out...
  He cried.

All quieting. Some sighing.
They fall to the ground. They're crying.

THE ELDERLY

What happens in the street we're seeing
Through half an opening of screening.

On strangers' kiddies kisses showered
And water for the window flowers.

We live our lives at God's disposal,
Disposing pages from the journal.

HOSPITAL GARDENS

Perceive this curious moment, inexpressible,
That usually in the afternoons goes down the street
On holidays—and wraps you in woe's stranglehold,
And in your heart you feel a monumental need.

You see the people's boredom and despondent streets,
Anxious from the quiet, woeful separations,
And in your soul awakens a gentle lethargy:
The evangelistic gloom of hospital gardens.

...A bell will call from somewhere steadily, routinely,
On naked trees—the nests of solitary swallows,
The widow's sorrows, apathy, orphans from nurseries,
Someone's uncomely mourning, refuge for the old folks...

Perceive this curious moment... People in their houses,
Dry and tidy streets... From somewhere a song of misfortune...
And with no one to witness, how you feel such sadness,
Like the student who is last to leave the classroom.

SYMPHONY OF AGES

Bangs the age old symphony, the solemn anthem:
Burrowing tough lumps of earth with piercing plowers,
Clinking steely blades of silvery separation,
On the anvil fall the bangs of heavy hammers.

They beat the war drums! Harder! Fear defines the meter!
A million strings are echoing the spreading anthem,
Roads are darkening with crowds of dusty clusters,
As the savage stomps of Hunnish horse hooves hasten.

Cities burning! Rome ablaze in bloody shimmer
For pleasure of the Caesars! For the drunken princes!
Fears of dying! Crying elders, drowned out by clamor,
A panicked fuss in the delirious monstrous fortress!

With Christs on crucifixes! Wood heaps burning!
Mournful miserere... —Smell of burning corpses!
Women! Bloodshed! Bread! And gold! Colossi collapsing
To stony debris with a wallop! Sodom! Day of judgement!

Hey, harder! Sharper! Harsher! Bang the walls with axes!
Engine boilers bursting! Revolution! Slaughter!
Elemental cataclysms! Wars! Disasters!
Dark prison bolts are screeching! Lusty masses scatter!

Roars the Symphony of Ages! The song astounds!
Mad in its perilous rush! No limits! Never done!
—Hey, Earth! And then my singing spirit will resound:
"Go racing round the Sun, the Sun, the Sun, the Sun!!"

ATTACK

"Hooray!" Like herds of buffalo, their brains abandoned,
Doubled over—forward onto bayonets they're plunging!
Drunk with blood, with flame, with clamoring and cannons,
Wrathful, delightful, like horses to the finish lunging.

Creaking Gatling guns compactly, dryly crackle,
Sweeping people in a quick uptick commotion,
Something breaks—and in the face an iron sparkle,
Whirling lifeless corpses, bloody fleshy mountain.

They got him! Bayonets are kicking, ripping, biting
Bellies, breasts and faces, warm blood empties,
With heavy boots they crush the faces of the dying
Or with their load they trample over bloody bellies.

Finally, their feet in dark blood puddles tarry,
Sweaty, from their deadly dancing torn asunder,
—Like madmen who bring flowers to the mortuary,
On the conquered rampart they array their banner.

HOW VERSE ARISES

Lyric strangeness. Lyric zone.
Shh... The soul awaits occasion,
That elusive "something" (emotion
And style of feeling, style and tone...)

And then—a word. The first of words
Flashes through the mind then flying
Hits the very heart of styling,
And tells the soul: speak on, be heard!

And then—a storm! Then—lunacy!
Flash of order overpowering!
And then—an ease. The head is bowing
Simply sobbing... sobs so sweet...

PEACHES

Do you hear? There's juiciness in this word, there's acrid sweetness of crushed fruit slush: juice, eruption drunken greedily by lusting lips.

Tender, globular, with softly mossy fluff, this peach it lures me, wakening craving, I must caress it with my lips, grip it lightly in my fingertips, caressingly stroke and blow the velvety down. A pity it's not all pinkishly pristine like in this—look—place… The peach is warm tucked in my hands, so soft now that the juice will let go any moment, I'm drunk on this, this thing of lips… O flowery flesh! O juices, sent circling through the tree, moved by the mysterious Force of Life! The juice that plumps the fetus in the warmth of spring and sun! I drink the drink, I crush, I'm sucking!…

Did I kiss your lips?

BETRAYAL

And why is it you favor him, you curious, callous girl? He's cold, colorless, like a suicidal corpse he is... Do not embarrass me. Already shepherds point their fingers at you, and the priest would like to curse you from the pulpit.

How did I know? You think I had not seen how you were running in the evening on a wet meadow over a woodland spring, overgrown with mint and forget-me-nots? Your nymphish body slipped from thin linens and wispy nudity nestled in the moss, crushing blueberries. O how your arms thrashed in the air! O how they grasped at him! You were saying something heated, rapid, secret, devoted—but in some alien language, one known to toadstools or common to shamans:

"Árgile, árgile, tivio-tila, tija, tija!"

You swallowed him with your swanlike swathing, you village Leda from a white cottage, overgrown with wilding vine.

...And you returned again at edge of night, illicitly smiling, nakedly...

Glossy Your body with silver lunar glaze. From heated embraces your cold and colorless lover has melted.

I know the truth, that you betray me with the moon.

Hey, beware, before I catch you.

LILY

I pulled apart the closed up lily petals and showed her the flower's demure interior.

—Stop, let it be.

Not knowing yet, but having a sense of it, I laughed abruptly and abruptly stopped short...

—Because?...

Her eyes were electric and secret, narrowed, indecisively answering...

Then from four sides I opened wide the white lily body, and dripping lips caressed inside...

And when I raised my eyes, she was ablush, her bosom undulant and pupils brilliant.

And smiling slightly (probably at my lips, dyed yellow from the pollen)—in a specially stirring, shaking voice she tells me:

—Lord you are so-phis-ti-ca-ted-ly obscene!...

from

Socrates Dancing
1920

OUR WISDOM

How shall I indoctrinate you with this wisdom?
We were quiet people, with our simple rhythms.

With our simple rhythms, folk uneducated,
Baptized by the word-flame, word-flame instigated.

Weaving words we slyly reach a rhymed refraining,
Blooming—sunshine, sunlight—blossoms in its naming.

Yet within our speech, in its peculiar splendor,
Worlds are called just as they are, with perfect candor.

Without books or teachings, but in silent musings,
By ourselves alone we've figured out a few things:

Of those nighttime moments, dashing through the vastness,
Seeing shadows never knowing what has cast it.

On the earth we stay perpetually youthful,
In our garden gleaming Harbinger will circle.

And the day we die we shall surrender humbly
Unto God what's Caesar's, unto God what's holy.

VANITAS

All the vain vanity. The soul, the data,
The vastness of God's work, the fragile infants,
The finished deeds so boastfully audacious,
The lovely arcane words and mad opinions.

All the vain vanity! The ages, hours
Continuing their purposeless parading.
Deaf infinity eternally mother
To sunrises and sunsets—daily, daily.

With just the lasting Truth of Christ everlasting
In a single flash of GOODNESS—all is conscious!
Gone—my mad mistakes, my sweet entrapping:
Vanitas vanitatum et vanitas omnia.

DIALOGUE

If in the whitest, whitest grove the prophets gather,
   What sort of grove?
         —Sacred...

If flower blossoms, blossoms in the midnight hour,
   What flower grows?
         —Secret...

If star is trembling trembled dreams about the ocean,
   What are these dreams?
         —Quiet...

If I am crying, crying for You, my devotion,
   What tears are these?
         —Tragic...

Abyss, where love descends the depths obliterated,
   What's this abyss?
         —Heinous...

For You a sorrow—tragic, quiet, secret, sacred,
   What sorrow's this?
         —Jesus!...

WORN DOWN BY FRENZIED TEMPESTS...

> *"Mais, vrai, j'ai trop pleuré!"*
> —Rimbaud

Worn down by frenzied tempests, like a drunken vessel,
There's nothing more I long for, only splendid silence
And someone who will fathom my unspoken trouble,
Someone who will distinguish my unnamed desires.

Someone whose brilliant spirit will pervade my hours,
That after all the anguish I might know God's respite,
Someone whose hands of mercy touch me with the power
To navigate a raging heart toward the quiet.

I'm coming for my silence. For my bliss. Who's waiting?
Which way then? Ah, the blindness! You should simply—journey.
I know I'm bound to get there with the path I'm taking,
Because my paths all lead to You eventually.

LITANY

I'm praying, Lord, passionately,
I'm praying, Lord, sincerely,
For the suffering embarrassed,
For the trembling expectant,
For the dead's elusive resurgence,
For the dying's helplessnesses,
For misapprehended sadness,
For hopeless supplications,
For the ridiculed, offended,
For the foolish, downtrodden, and villains,
For those who are running winded
To the very nearest physician,
For those who return from the cities
Coming home with hearts unsteady,
For the inadvertent rudeness,
For being booed on stages,
For the tedious, hideous, graceless,
For the powerless, vanquished, molested,
For those who may not be sleeping,
For those who are frightened of dying,
For those in pharmacies waiting,
For the tardy whose trains are departing,
—FOR ALL THE PLANET'S PEOPLE,
For their difficulties, worries,
Anxieties, misgivings,
For restlessness and grieving,
Desiring, not succeeding,
For every little twitching,
That isn't glad rejoicing,

Which should forever be shining
Upon these people kindly—
I'm praying, Lord, sincerely,
I'm praying, Lord, passionately!

BEGGARS' FROST

Biting frost insinuates our shredded garments,
Wind-lined winter coats, with holes for every squall,
We tuck our freezing ears into our cutoff collars,
Desperately pressing into jagged walls.

And what are we to bring you, you the warm and fragrant,
The capricious, pampered, beauteous beloved?
Ragged, chilly hands? Blue faces that have stiffened?
Or tattered rags that winter frost has frozen solid?

Maybe blistered lips or maybe ruddy noses?
Maybe quickly palpitating, rigid corpses?
Or bewildered eyes, that leak like water hoses,
Insufferably dribbling their salty droplets?

Glassy wind will cut your face with snowflake spillage,
Lashing out the whoosh and pain like sharpened brushes,
And frost with predatory talons pinches, pinches,
Maliciously the burning needle nudges, nudges.

Breathe and blow upon your fingers! Lips need rubbing!
How we're shivering and groaning in petrified agony!
Our legs now numb, they beat upon the ground, start jumping
To dance, to dance and holler till our teeth are clattering.

And at the wall a dancing rhythm now commences,
Impatient hopping, frolicking hysterically,
Rags shiver over all the frigid, morbid corpses,
Wind disperses an ecstatic revelry.

We cross ourselves our arms convulsing in a frenzy
As our legs, possessed, are dancing ever faster,
Crackling frost exploding fiery and fiercely
Until it melts in warmth, in senseless blissful rapture.

And behind our backs the frosted walls will soften
To give us refuge in their warm and lustful bodies,
Like a lover's skin, that's ticklish as satin,
A caressing pleasure suddenly is raging!

And we wallow in the warmth of feather bedding,
In spasms of sweet dancing we are burning naked,
Down into the sultry milk bath we're descending
With braided bodies seething, lovingly vivacious!

Into our shredded purple veins derangement decants
A concentrated sweet liqueur, a golden streaming,
By breathing forest heat, into the trees we'll graft
Where sticky meaty cactuses are interweaving.

We're basking in the lecherous Sahara desert,
We're digging in the entrails of the bloody lionesses,
We're frying just like pork rinds in the solar swelter
And in the streets we drip a grease that's incandescent!

We are no more! What's left is just the furious dances!
A scorching wind swept us away in torrid pleasure!
—Look! Upon the whitened wall there's baked-in traces;
Blood where dance dissolved to walls for frosty beggars!

SOCRATES DANCING

Roasting in sunbeams, me the old drifter...
Yawning, stretching and reclining.
Old perhaps, but showing vigor:
From the cup I quickly swigger,
Vocalizing.

Sunbeams heating my old skeleton
And clever, gray-haired, shaggy noggin,
In clever noggin, like woods in their prime,
Buzzes and buzzes the cleverest liquor,
Eternal thinking river, river,
Like time.

What are you staring at, Cyrbeus?
What do you think? Of this ole ignoramus,
Now that his jabbering's come to an end,
Now that he's spilled the beans? Yes, yes...
Go, bake your bread.

Disciples in the alleys grinning,
That now the master's head is spinning,
That Socrates got drunk...
Go, Cyrbeus, tell all disciples,
That now I've hit the heart of matters:
That it's a virtue—licking dust
From Athens' streets! Or tell disciples,
That it's a virtue—bladder bluster!
A virtue—pouring water from pitchers!
Or—let it spill over! Whatever...

And if you wish—come sit here close,
Don't bake your loaves, don't bake your crescents,
Just sip yourself here in my presence,
Come toast with me now, toast!

What is it now? You're sorry, Cyrbeus,
That my tongue's a twisted twitter?
That I'm grinning so, my Cyrbit,
That in the daytime Athens market,
I lie like a beggar, sipping liquor?
For a sage, you say, it's unbecoming,
Teaching such a sorry lesson:
Old men romping
Like children?
That I don't congregate disciples,
That routes to truth I've not identified,
Don't counsel,
Don't philosophize?
Ah yes… ah yes…

Evil! Good! —truth? Gods and people,
Virtue, eternity, words and actions,
And from the beginning—new iterations,
Gods and people, evil, good,
Republicanism, words and actions,
Beauty! This-that-this again!…
My dear—derisions!

You have heard from Heriphona,
That I'm the wisest one… So spake
The oracle, extolled persona,
My brow is glowing from all the festooning!
Well witness what the wisest is doing:

O!
For what's a word, and what's an action?
For what is good, and what is not?
When getting drunk on gold concoctions,
When my head's shaggy as a dog
And in my head a chaos crashes?!
Witness how the philosopher dances:
And hop-hop-hop, and hop-hop-hop!
And hopping, hopping, hop-hop-hop!
Witness how the wisest dances!
How ancient legs will leap and scuttle,
Good and evil, gods and people,
Virtue, truth, eternal Fortune,
Hopping, hopping, goes the pattern:
One on the right side—hop-hop-hop!
One of the left side—hop-hop-hop!
Hippity hoppity, come on, Xanthippe!
The music plays on!

And come along as well, my Cyrbit,
Yes, let's go around the market,
The sage is dancing, let's go on a journey
Virtue, truth and gods and beauty,
Witness, people, witness, gapers,
Xanthippe will lambaste me later,
All within me twitches nonstop,
And I've become a hop-hop-hop!
Yes endlessly, until I die
Let the bright sky writhe and writhe,
Yes—from the top, let's have more bopping,
Again the bacon's hopping, hopping!
Don't pity these old legs one bit!
Let God the great be glad for it,

That Socrates divined the truth,
That now he knows! Knows through and through!
That he has reached the farthest expanses,
He—the wisest, he—advances,
The drifter ugly as a dog
Knew the dances, knew the dances,
Hopping, hopping, hop-hop-hop!!!

TWO WINDS

First of winds—through fields it blows,
Second wind—plays in the grove:
Quietly and delicately,
Rustles and caresses leaves,
Then slows...

First of winds—a rushing rascal!
Flippant vaulting, falling flatly,
Leaping, gusting, escalating,
Into mountains excavating,
Toppling over and collapsing
Onto sleepy, rustling trees,
Where with quiet delicacy
Rustles and caresses leaves
The second wind...

Cherry blossoms stir like snow,
Snickering throughout the grove,
Joining now his windy brother,
Comrades through the fields of summer,
Both go chasing birds and billows,
Racing, tangling up in windmills,
Causing all its sails confusion,
Leftward, rightward, whoosh, convulsions,
Lungs let loose with all their might,
Pranksters, breezily defiant!...

And in the grove it's quiet, quiet...

MY LIFE

Blood, dreams, hastes, needs,
Peaks, clouds, quakes, sparks,
Tears, blinks, buds, beams,
Sobs, stars, fears, frost— —!
    O, my life!
    O, my life!
Take, lose, wane, waste,
Fun, wrath, mad, flight!
Live! dream! sob! quake!
Rush, fly, dash, ride!
    O, my life!!
    O, my life!!
Ache? Death? Sure, sure!
See, see: charmed tricks!
None, none! Day—bird!
Flit! flight! whirl! whiz!
    O, life, my life!

from

The Seventh Autumn
1922

NAME

Life for me once had a name—a maiden's,
Name clear as first lilies of the valley,
Picked from grasses glistening at dawning
By those lilied hands so Chopinescent.

With this name were woven many sunbeams,
Shone on rustling forest vegetation,
Maytime lilac trees bedewed, pearlescent,
With this name they're fragrant as your darling…

And when heaven emptied in the evening,
Quiet from the field blew through the highland,
In warm breezes and in swallow mayhem,
In each tree that very name was seething.

…Smoke throughout the opal twilight misting
Formed a gauzy cloud and then it vanished,
Melancholy mournful spirit chanted:
How had I for such a name been living?

ANGRY POEM

You didn't know. That it was raining
And I was wandering the street,
And was searching, and was waiting
In hostile, horrid hungering.

You didn't know. That I was angry.
And I went and started drinking:
Vodka, cognac, vodka, cognac,
And I was beaming, yes beaming!

Look: this is a lousy poem,
Full of wrathfulness and angry,
For the searching, for the waiting
In the pouring autumn evening.

FATHERLAND

My fatherland is God,
Ghost, Son and cosmic Father.
Whichever road I'm on
Towards him the spirit flutters.

My fatherland's a field,
Field Polish, heartfelt, simple,
My Lord, there may you yield
A morsel for rest eternal.

My fatherland is home,
Beloved home of childhood,
Where quiet dreams may roam
Like cherubs in a wildwood.

I'm looking, spent and shot,
In thy pure eyes of azure,
And there is all: there's God,
And Poland, and home of fathers.

from

The Fourth Volume of Poems
1923

DEATH

Like a razor through butter, through the mind it will pass;
Like a stone into water—softly: splash...

WE—PEOPLE

We people are a bloodstained congregation,
Because we seized fierce fires from the heavens.

We rub ourselves in life lasciviously!
O fleshy days! You round commodity!

How hard the veins with their distended bellies.
We ride the galloping days as if they were fillies.

We gnaw the world within our mouths like cherries,
Like twenty cherries simultaneously.

Bodies bulging full of pulp and moisture,
Flaunted for desirable stingers.

And with the pulpy juices overriding,
We go crazy from the golden biting.

INSTRUCTION

They instructed me with lots of wisdom,
Logarithms, formulas and patterns,
Quadrangles and triangles and pistons,
They instructed me ad infinitum.

Recitations on the "natural wonders,"
Demonstrated panoplies of secrets:
On a slide "the life in drops of water,"
On another—"all the lunar trenches."

Limitless supply of information:
$2\pi R$ and acid that's sulfuric,
Apples, radiation, Crookes and Newton,
H_2, N_2, changing atmospherics.

I have seen the sphere with ice within it,
Seen that rubbing amber cedes electrons...
When a body is immersed in liquid
It will lose as much as it... et cetera.

In another hemisphere I fathom
Sunlight shines, while we exist in darkness!
Different items crammed into my noggin,
Dazzling instruction that is pointless.

And nothing do I know, my sense is hopeless,
I still believe with my mistaken notions,
People in the hemisphere below us
Must be upside down in all their motions.

Till this day I still have schoolboy terrors:
God will snatch me—I'll be standing speechless!
—Lord, my God! I do not know the answers,
I… excuse me please, this headache's vicious…

Vexing lesson. Right away I couldn't.
But I'm learning… and if I could ask you…
Please! A second life could I be given,
Like a second year in this same classroom.

RECKONING

Some are counting me throughout the evening,
Writing and writing, and still just a trifling.
Jumping clumsy cyphers.
I am already weak and weary,
Trillions, quadrillioncy,
Everlasting line of teeming
Figures.
They cannot, no, they cannot count me,
They're wrong, they're scrawling in a frenzy,
Somewhere skulks a dumb mistake.
So back again to the beginning,
Above my glutted head are hanging
Numbers in maggoty ranks.

A billion billions they have reckoned,
Multiplied by a hundred million,
Still threatening, still terrorizing,
That by 13 they'll multiply me,
By my infinity of dolor,
They then will raise me to the power,
17th, 19th, and even higher,
More raising and more multiplying,
Numbers up to heaven piling,
Universe bursts, into the vastness,
Over my poor head the massive
Pyramids and abracadabras,
Hundred-century columns collapsing,
Like cooties scattered into crannies,

Depleted then again enhancing
In two, in fours, in fives, in eighties,
In sevens, zeroes and three sixties,
Swelling swarms of hundred-trillions,
Sixes, billions—octillions,
Descends on me a starving army,
Till they count me, till they tally,
Till black hangmen multiply us
By all the worlds and universes.

IN THE FOREST

On slippery roots unyielding,
On moss profound and velvety,
Anthill ferociously teeming:
Mound convulsing in misery.

Throughout the treetop glosses,
Wet and warm from rainfall,
Smelling of fungus softness,
Branches creak and crackle.

And then—pouring down—on fir trees
The sunlight gushing, streaming,
And follows the cheeping-chirping,
Chirruping, sadly weeping...

Chir-tri-o-tru-li-tro-so-wing,
Songs from the summits hastened,
Birds their beaks are moistening,
Their throats rinsed by the heavens!

Everything dripping with glowing,
The touch of bark is syrupy,
—And the anthill ferociously foaming:
Mound convulsing in misery.

SLAUGHTERED BIRCHES

I'll open the birch veins with a hatchet,
Through flesh I'll slash, through root I'll hack it.
I'll soak in the sticky plasma of birches,
With white wounds my mouth converges.

My snatchy teeth sink into birch trunk,
My greedy lips drink up the juices.
Straight from the bark my mouth will pillage
The core tormented with my kisses.

Maybe these drugs from the living tree
Will teach me the words, the words I will need:
Glory to summer, glory to birch,
From lunatic lips, to God's universe!

from
Words in Blood
1926

WORD AND FLESH

I

The word became flesh embodied
And amongst us made his dwelling,
I'm feeding a ravenous body
Words as if they were berries;
I drink as if cold water
Words with my mouth, voracious,
I breathe them in like weather,
I crumple them like young verdure,
I rub them with sweet fragrance.

The word is wine and honey,
The word is meat and pastry,
Words my eyes are leading
Through starry skyway journeys.
Joy of sacred gifting,
O! cherished ever after!
Words for my daily living
Give me today, my Master!

II

I have but one activity:
I am just a hunter of words.
Vigilant and listening
I hunt throughout the world.

With words the moments flutter,
And all that I loved and perceived,
All day long will mutter
In a swarm of sunning bees.

The wingèd words will nick me,
Their stingers cut to blood,
Piercing, words injecting
The sweetest buzz.

The heart holds flitting
Words in captivity,
That's why hearts careen.
Bewitched by honey
The head is spinning,
That's why—the dream.

III

Each word has roots within the dark of earth's abysses,
And when it springs to surface—then its green slips out,
Another intertwines along its fibrous freshness,
And linking limbs together upwards they will sprout.

Into head and shoulders earthblood wordsurge gushes:
It opens up our arms, our head is wet and sunlit.
Ah, in the springtime flutter, in the oakwood forests,
Where upon twin limbs the songbird sings full-hearted.

Day, like from a womb, emerges from the darkness
And that day starts living, youthful and prodigious,
And seizes us for hours, like in love's embraces,
And kisses, squeezing words straight out the mouth, like juices.

This is the way of passion, of twitchy screaming pleasure,
Bloodied by the blow of God, like a caesarian:
Heads, severely severed by the sunlight cleaver,
Wombs, ripped of their words, like mothers of their children.

IV

You surely are my redness,
You surely are my greenery.
Brains in nervated branches:
Plants within living beings.

A world of ferocious oppression,
God of horrific momentum,
In the brain the noise of a poison,
Words, the liquified mayhem.

Blood of mine—my parlance,
Pulp that's ardent, earthen.
—Reddens, green turns, are words,
Of the rebellious anthem!

V

Not for nothing that sung rhymes with blood,
Not for nothing that blood recalls grudge.
Words know just which ringing rushes!
Blood—that's sung—with grudges.

Our grudges tear the heavenly roof,
Melting words in a fiery soup,
And a light shines down and exposes
God in the flesh, in the poets!

RUSH

Scent of peppermint by the water,
tuft of bulrushes undulated,
dawn was pinkening, water swaggered,
gust through mint and rush cascaded.

I did not know then that these grasses
would appear as words in poems years after
nor that I'd conjure across the expanses,
instead of just lying by water and flowers.

I did not know that I'd be so haggard,
searching for words for the world and its clatter,
I did not know when you kneel by the water,
that then you must suffer many years after.

I only knew that in the bulrushes
were long, resilient, slender fibers,
I wove them in a wispy gossamer,
which netted quantities of nothingness.

God of my good adolescence,
holy God of my bright dawning!
Will life no longer be allotting
scenes by the pond with minty fragrance?

And so it always goes—of course it does—
That I elicit words from anguish,
and bulrushes, the simple bulrushes
I simply nevermore shall witness.

LET WORDS DRAW BLOOD!

Your words are like parlor puppies,
And mine—like rabid dobermans!
Damn your arabesquing and burlesquing
And—rather than placing dashes and ellipses—
Smack with your poems,
Hammer their heads in!
Rip up, tear to tatters
Your sonnets and triolettas.
Simpletons!
Let poetry be abhorrent
To flat and flaxen
Lascivious virgins!
Let words draw blood—like chopping off noggins!
O words! Words sharpened and golden!
Predacious and potent,
Like lions! Like lions!

BOOTS

My muddy loafers, like two mangy mutts, I place
At the edge of the bed to stand guard through the evening.
I sleep lifelessly, with the moon's silver scar on my face,
Above a wet boot an arm is dangling serenely.

At night swollen clouds across the ceiling stray,
Like tears, steps echo through the lonely chamber:
My tortured trudgers sleep in a fevered splatter
And drag on me, they drag like through the rain.

Come morning, sunlight's flooded all the flooring
And light of day will hurl at me my shame:
Teeth with wooden heels are waiting for me,
Horrid dry boots that hunger for my pain.

THE APARTMENT

Everything is all a lie:
Four illuminated rooms
And these fixtures, of which I speak—all mine,
And these flowers, of which I speak—alive,
Everything is all a lie.
And when I walk the steps—they are not mine.
I float in a foggy dream from room to room.

I was fetched here from infinity
By gray and cloudy seas.
When on the couch I lean,
Vast spinning prehistory encircles me,
When I fall asleep—I fall into the deep,
And eyes open wide to see,
From dream to apartment escapes the cascade
Of looming, humming eternity.

COCKTAIL

Spiral viperine of sugared verdure
Nimbly slithered in golden wallow
Lord of Jazz and Cocktail, Mister Mixer,
My Governor of Colorgrogo.

Then a bloody drop dripped from the bottle,
Then gurgled, buckled in a rainbow.
Streak of grass deep in the golden vodka
Pinkening with spider spangles.

And when everything was seething color,
Squirt of wine and sprinkle of arrack,
Until inside the glass emerged a flutter
Of a fretful, colorful parrot.

Leisurely he topples over, circles,
Fluid, sleepy, waffling rover,
Paints with jangling colored triangles,
In the bottle's glaze—my eyes glass over.

And suddenly beneath the light I faced him,
How he floundered and foamed, and was glowing,
Governor who wore the snow white apron
His face had peacocks and hummingbirds showing.

And with a gulp the colors went down the barrel,
As if I had swallowed the heavens over me,
Every single cork deployed a salvo
From the mind of My Poetic Glory!

REPORT ON THE TRIP TO THE EXHIBITION OF DECORATIVE ARTS IN PARIS

There is in this Paris
Much shouting and debauchery,
And this
"Exposition des Arts Décoratifs."
I'm sitting in some joint in the vicinity
Drinking an apéritif,
The fifth one or the sixth.

On the walkway
In a braided seat
I'm chatting away
With a green tree:
—Arbre! Ecoutez!
Votre santé!
C'est vous—le plus beau pavillon polonais!

FANTASTIC STROLL THROUGH THE FOREST OF FONTAINEBLEAU

Through the gloomy forest stepping quick.
Chilly, noisy beneath the glistening foliage.
Pathway straight, as if jolted by a whip:
Lengthy barrel with a luminous orifice.

Forest weeps with wind. A leaf fell low.
Worried birds are wailing. It will be raining.
This I know: you must go, you must go
Into the mad green forest hastening.

Circle widens. I know what it will hold,
In the distance, blustering and sprinkling:
Golden rainfall and sunny smoke
Steaming, dewy in the clearing.

Might there be a miracle of God,
Such that time and space escape their arrow,
And the forest roads get all mixed up,
And well—look: my hometown meadow!

BACK THEN

Back when cinema was still called "bioscope"
Or "illusion,"
Back when I wore the cap of a pupil,
Everything truly was illusion,
Dreaminess and jovial.

"Cunard" and "White Star" were beyond my understanding,
I had in Lodz my enchanted tenement,
There was no need for any dollars then,
Because each landing
Was another ship deck.

Back when I was still writing: "Flower chalices"
And "rosy carpets,"
And I was rhyming:
—Quiet,
—Spirit,
I truly had a quiet spirit.

Back then,
Back when cinema was called "bioscope,"
Back when stairs housed curiosities,
Back when everything was song awakening in the throat,
I was even happier then.
Today I'm merely happy.

UNKNOWN TREE

*dedicated to the holiest memory
of Stefan Żeromski*

Where are you proud and powerful tree,
Branching outward, boisterous leaves,
Your roots all knotted, crowding the ground,
Tree that shall be a coffin for me?

I must meet you, knock on your bark,
Calling through forests, resounding in parks:
Where art thou, clandestine coffin tree?
Thy fiancé comes to play his part!

Roaming dark woods uneasily,
Still unable to find my tree,
Murmur for me, for our eternity,
Before I lie with you to sleep.

It must all be arranged in advance
Of those heavy, mortal challenges,
When we are judged eternally
To turn to ash, to sterile slabs.

Perhaps on a raft on gray-blue waves
You'll come ashore from far away,
And we'll be ashamed, my forever neighbor,
That not till death did we embrace.

Or perhaps you're growing before my home,
Greeted each day yet still unknown,
And someone perhaps has carved in your bark
Lovely letters on a heart enthroned?

Delightfully long we'd be jabbering,
Piqued by poetry, pushed into grief,
You'd press apart this blackened earth
To amaze the grave with new flowering.

You'd somehow implant me in your frame,
Seized from earth with a furtive rage!
Perhaps some rhizome links to a nerve
And we become tree above the grave!

Perhaps a great sighing from the womb
Will lift green earth into mountainous bloom,
The only earth, the native earth,
Whose very heart that tomb did wound.

from
The Czarnolas Matter
1929

THE SOURCE

From the cold spring you draw diamantine water
With a pitcher, green and earthen.
Within it sky was blueish melted weather,
Drowning in depths of white cloud linen.

Head is warm under blessed gracious sunlight,
Hands at rest in clear depths of coolness.
Golden heat drifts down the country roadside
And will spread throughout the lupins.

There is within the pitcher, green and earthen,
Iron cold water—you imbibe it.
A fragrant, heated wave comes from the lupins,
You breathe it in, you lower your eyelids.

MATHEMATICS

Universal temple!
Refuge from demons disturbing my senses!
The only one true rock,
O eternal Eye that marks
And sees me without limits!

A number savior!
Arise! Become! And show me!
An unrelenting PATTERN
For seizing, renaming, controlling!

Here is a square. A square without elaboration.
This four-line prison circumscribing one thing only.
O acrid mathematics! You've given the world instruction!
You've taunted God and Devil, o you heretical cruelty!
Square the chaos precluding,
No poem could ever offer such perfection!

Here is the finity, the expertise, the finality,
The proud unicity of Law is overjoying,
That with four lines I introduced inevitability.
Nothing here *is happening*. Same case ongoing.

Jesus! If you had not had this burning bloodstream,
That you were whisked to heaven, to learn the truthful promise,
If you had pondered one day longer, silently, staunchly,
Straight lines into a figure you would have to harness
And not trouble us with the cross—but redeem us with the compass.

BAGDAD, OR ABOUT A FUTURE POET

A child is brimming with Bagdad on this winter evening,
Perhaps from the winding wallpaper? From the new book?
For down the wall cascades a colorful atrocity,
For out the book come swooping streaks of spotted birds.

The green and silken cord that carries electricity
Crawled in a dream with plant and reptile. And there it started:
Breeding in a backwoods basket, weaved, departed,
Writhed with tree beasts and the faces of the visiting.

Then—a murmur of shuffled cards. And then a fanning,
Like an aurora, figures in a semicircle.
Child swims through the terror of TRANSFIGURED happenings,
And quickly dreaming shapes a city on a table.

And when the messenger's red cap out in the street
Landed on the splendid eye of sleep, like a cataract,
The masses in the slanted city were whispering
And then the child awakened—shouting loudly: "Bagdad!"

Jumps up, looks at the window. There's the moon, a snippet
Standing barely green. On the horrid papered boundary
A dream goes through the shadowed cinema, crashing equipment,
And then the poor, poor child. The child then started crying!

For listen and take heed,
That under sacred order,
Whoever with word once fell in delusional dream,
This one shall not know happiness, not ever!

MELODY

Early autumn—season that beseems me.
Morning gray—the color of my vision.
Great café—I sit in seventh heaven,
I could stay like this till evening.

Past the windows so much sprinting,
But I don't hear them, I'm oblivious,
They fall away with autumn grinning,
Lulled I gaze into the distance.

The best: these mornings in the patisserie
And gazing as the street is passing.
Such mornings you become a lover,
And a sadder person, and younger.

From love, from tender memories
The day began lethargic and empty.
Those words that you've not written me
My grinning lips form into poetry.

And altogether it's a melody,
And melodious moments jointly flow.
A foreign lass in a checkered coat
Smilingly, splendidly orders "chocolaty."

Such a wispy, cloudy woman!
Such as us are so uncommon!
And such perfumes exploded!
And such a poet!...

ABOUT MY TABLE

Heavy grieving cube,
From crape myrtle wood,
Tucked against the wall
My table stands macabre.
If only it had tires
It'd be a hearse for hire,
If only it had strings
A piano it would be.
Miserable creature
With widened mouth—a drawer.
Lying down there, lying:
Snippets, stringlets, wraps, receipts,
Debris of times deceased,
Bits of the boring temporal,
Lying there, lying:
Someone's mortal struggle,
In drawer abiding,
Another's rustling dreams,
Sad whispered memories:
This one... that one... that other...
Fellowship of Fact Cadavers,
Unreachable by wordly matters.

A WORD ABOUT THE MOON IN THE POND

Moon plunges in the water,
Phosphoric drowning lights.
Night sorcerer the light churns over,
So every oily droplet shines.

CEILING

Bed seems like it's sinking. Dropping into crevices.
And sloshing in the depths there in the sedentary
Cesspit of continents, cyanotic expectorant—
—Final sea of sickness, steeply escalating.

So before the final delusion the pastor anoints them,
Bringing about some doubtful eternal consolation,
Reading ceiling ciphers like heaven from the chasm,
And the fallen flies are beaming grins of welcome.

Hospital Columbuses are drunk with whiteness,
Flowing through horrific oceanic spaces,
For long ago they grew impatient with their patience,
Too much tranquility at sea will make them anxious.

This sky together with the sea, and these white ceilings,
Steady navigating with no storm or harbor
And in the remains of a dreary life the catch is measly:
A speck of dark or scuff in the suspended nether.

Yes everything is Patmos prophetically repeated,
When the ragged dots upon the lime and gypsum
Form constellations that the sailor miscompleted
For he sees the albino beast, as in the Revelation.

from

The Gypsy Bible
1933

THE GYPSY BIBLE

The gypsy bible, what is it you think?
Unscripted, prophetic, migratory.
Whispered by silver night to her grannies,
Anointed in midsummer gleam.

With aroma of crushed myrtle,
Forest noise and star Kabbalah,
Shade of grave and stack of tarot,
Ancestral crypt and white phantasma.

Who uncovered this book? We, sages,
Rummaging ancient recollections.
Scent-driven, touched by premonition,
Gazing beneath the thoughts and senses.

Through the dales of forsaken lessons
Fairytales wind like a wriggling river:
Not in life, not in death, but between them,
For death and life are both enraptured.

At night upon this book the waxy
Teardrops fall from mourning tapers.
In this, the book of delusional fancy,
Dreams will topple over like pages.

Flashing vibration of versification,
You cannot capture the arcane,
Something like: the poet's martyrdom...
...that something be saved...
                        And the book melts away.

GRASS

Grass, grass up to the knees!
Raise yourself up to my temples,
Let all other thoughts leave
No more me, no more meadow.

Let me turn myself herby,
Stemmed to my bony essence,
No more need for discerning
Words twixt me and your freshness.

Whether you or me they address
A single name will do them:
Both of us either—grass.
Both of us either—tuwim.

SUM OF AUTUMN

Hours withering slowly. Weakening moment to moment:
This branch submerged in autumn. I'm gliding along upon it
In millimetered grief. A tiresome occupation.
From the day I knock off seconds. From the branch I knock off foliage.

And how shall I define the autumn? A deep exhalation:
Myself, a human, rising from the cool lake bottom.
Hands through the window dipped in the lake of day and autumn.
A chill leaps through them. Rain drizzles. Knocking off foliage and moments.

MUSE

The wife of the pharmacist in curlers,
Rosy, hefty, with a snub nose,
Singing all morning her high voice crows
O *My Longing*'s romantic verses.

Her robe is feathered, her dog is bristling
In the shabby froth of its white tendrils,
Her thoughts—in bed with the king of tenors,
When coffee splashes on the sheepskin.

Harsh limestone embers over gutters
Lie low and dusty in dry combustion,
And she—all trills and curls and ribbons,
And she—in a cloud of fluff she flutters.

Thus a yeast cake placed in the oven
Swells and grows into fragrant pastry.
So the pharmacist's wife has risen
With O *My Longing* over the city.

—Yellowing husband, pharmacy heron,
Pecking at the Latin prescriptions!
Above the heavens of your city
I'm floating after the plump muse singing.

MAYTIME TOIL

You must love come Maytime season,
Like an idiot, like a simpleton,
Suffering, dying, not knowing the reason,
Not for yourself, but for the passion.

Tangled up in the lilac frolics,
You must enmesh in dewy thickets
And with a sniff your head will swing
Jostling the bustling merry spring.

Long nights loving in the garden,
Then a stroll through solitude's gloom,
Slowly, sadly, for that's how it happens
After the funeral of our youth.

And following the hearse progressing
Bedecked in happy green fluorescing,
Mumbling nonsense preternatural,
Nonsense that is incomparable.

TO THE COMMON MAN

Next time the walls are freshly pasted
with declarations starting to stick,
when "for the soldiers," "for the masses"
sound the alarm with bold black print
and any thug, and any urchin
finds timeless lies they can believe in,
that you must go to pound the cannons,
murder, plunder, burn and poison;
when they begin their thousand prayers
to wrest the homeland to declension
and delude with colorful banners,
and induce for "historical reasons"
of glory, borders and expanses,
of fathers, grandfathers and standards,
of liberators and of martyrs;
with bishop, pastor, rabbi pressing
to give your bayonet a blessing,
God whispered to him the command,
that you must fight for the fatherland;
with bloodthirsty bastards busting over
all the front pages in screaming letters,
and wild mobs of hags—with flowers
start to shell them at "our soldiers."—
—O my unenlightened friend,
my fellow man from this or that land!
know who beats the bells of anxiety
the sovereigns with the lordly bellies;
know this common hoax they mount,
when they holler: "Guns to shoulders!"
that somewhere they found oil in the ground
and they'll be harvesting the dollars;

that something in their banks was wanting,
that somewhere they sniffed easy money
or the fatcat scumbags plotting
some way to raise the cotton duty.
Cast the rifle to the pavement!
Blood for you, and oil for bastards!
Throughout the capitals proclaim it,
Holler to defend your bloodshed:
"We get the game now, noble masters!"

from
The Burning Essence
1936

FORTY SPRINGS

Forty springs have swollen
Like forty green waterways
In one movement, one course, one cascade,
And snagged my expanding age.

Forty roaring springs,
A frothy youthful flood
With the voice of May it sings,
A bloated sack of love
Carried by springtime conceit
With the roots of trees,
With the shards of shattered paddles,
With the snippet of a mane,
That has gone to waste
When some silver splattered lion gave it to the spring,
Green chaos of forest cavities,
Torn by the jubilant tempest of blood unbridled
(Blood that's tarred and green!),
And trunks, like mammoth tusks, uprooted,
Streaming, coursing, convoluted—
Everything, everything
On crests of waves
Of forty swollen springs,
Dancing like dinghies urged to sea
By the spur of one desire,
Everything, everything
In one dark moment I carry,
One moment squeezed from the center
Of my forty swollen springs.

THE BLIZZARD

to Józef Wittlin

Lethargy dense like snow and snowlike circulates
Spinning flakes of snowy sleepiness around
My directionless day, my nonsensical age
And these disordered steps of mine upon the ground.

If I wish, I can sleep; if I wish, I can stand,
I can sit there by the window with last week's paper,
Or walk into lethargy—then not me, but another man,
Sitting by the window, will see a distant stranger.

Is it right or wrong: to fall asleep like this in the mist?
Whispering some snowy, foreboding, tardy tidings?
Is it right or wrong: to be a spinning shadow against
A circling snowstorm in an age with little lighting?

A snow duvet fell over me, an hour escaped
In whitest slumber, in fluffy, dusty, easy strides.
My directionless day, my nonsensical age
I offer to slow verse as sacrifice.

AND SO IT WAS...

And so it was, in dusky darkness
A living bud crawled out the branches
To come unstuck, to wailing songbirds,
At dawn—he sighed. And so it started.

For nearly an hour he satsmoldered,
Leisurely dozing in springtime ardor.
Then dragged outside the sticky socket
By flowery fowls increasingly louder.

For nearly an hour he did feather,
Seeing all the garden color.
Then pulled along the softest tether
By wings of breezes increasingly sweeter.

O see how they fight for your affections,
Merging into a motley ruckus:
Birds atwitter increasingly tender.
Increasingly zealous flower fragrance!

Nameless one you're then divided
By one force into two wonders,
And the branch from which you sprouted,
Anxiously beneath you shudders.

Then who? Then how? A coldness blowing.
The bird? The bloom? The buzz is dying,
And from the frightened heart of the planet
An existential dread is rising.

Then I picked him from the branches,
Like the firstborn from a fruit tree:
Such very sweetly scented breathing,
So very sadly singing poetry.

DISTANT TIGER

You can't see it from here, clearly,
You can't hear it naturally,
Like a cunning tiger creeping
Through the tropic understory.

When it's active, streaks of blackness
Lacerate the forest meshes
And then languorous from prowess
Goldly shines amongst the greenness.

There a flash then clatter, murmur,
Swarms of shredded leaves all over,
But from here you will not see it,
Naturally you will not hear it.

Here is quiet, here is calmness,
Wool in window, door with deadlock,
These four corners, I a fifth one,
And a cigarette, a teapot.

Here it's blissful, here's for drowsing,
One day clear, today it's cloudy,
Only sometimes in the darkness
Tiger blood before me flashes:

He was laying low and leaping
In this moment, just this second!
And you're shocked that on occasion
My eyes writhe with apprehension.

And you're shocked, surprised that sometimes
Through me shoots a sudden current,
You will then proceed to question
Why I'm quivering and ashen!

EARLY SPRING

Grayish season, without pleasure,
From blue darkness stripes of showers,
And all over you will wander
Sadly circling for an hour.

Walking you are but a shadow
Loathsome noiselessness entrances.
O the promise! O the sorrow!
Sparrows strung upon the branches.

Wailing briskly, feverishly,
They recite continuously
This and that among the birdies,
Unimaginable tidings.

What about? About: your craving
These old tales of sparrow scrapping,
Always circling, always waiting...
What for? For this. You see? Exactly.

EMPTY APARTMENT

Never leave your apartment on its own. Not because it may be robbed. For quite a different, little known reason.

Nothing can describe the rigid and focused grieving of an apartment when we are not home.

The clock, conductor of the void, wavers sixty times a minute whether to throw itself from the wall into the abyss of frozen time or to persevere.

Furniture keep quiet concerning the most venomous gossip about us. Sometimes they sigh, they creak, and return to silence.

I believe that during our absence, not just anyone uses the apartment as a love nest. Believe me that the spookiest orgies take place, events missed by mirrors which, while living and at home, we call: None, Nondescript, Not any, No one.

Shrouds and covers fly like in a seance. At best they're departing. Glass in the cupboard overflowing with triumphant nothing. Books, as ever, upright; essential, strictly feudal.

But they too, i.e. lines at one time living fonts, start sickly fermenting with the gray pustules of mortal murmurs.

Don't ask about what's in the drawers and dressers. Can you hear how those two words will whisper?

Verily, verily I say unto thee: better that thieves and vandals plunder your property than that hour, to be feared, when leaving your apartment empty.

* * *

With the last crumbs of youth—what to do? Disperse them to birds?
They could be dispersed to birds, they could be put into words.
Flying off, rapturous, coming back to gather new ones,
Coming back—the words, the birds—both afloat on winged hopes.

And what shall you tell them? No more! Poor things, there shall be no more.
Do they leave? No they don't believe it. And through the cloudy night
By the window they'll wait, they will beat their wings upon the panes
And will tumble, deceased and faithful. Both the birds and the words.

ERRATUM

A grim error crept into my life:
Hence the dark setting and complex text.
Kindly correct:
In year 40 from the top,
And somewhere there in the terrain below,
Instead of: despair
It should be: love.

TO GOD

Lord! Though they are sure to seize all things in sight,
To bind in steely chains in the forges of their vigor,
You shall continue rolling in abundant tides
In the cherished heart of the incidental drifter.

There is your fatherland and country of infancy,
First formation of a smile and swaying sleep,
There, o Joyful Father, in liquid golden strings
A sphere of sun is splashing tangled with the reeds.

And when those pretenders acting in your name
Roar into megaphones the winning legislation,
You—the scent of beauty, you—the bluish flame—
You wield, intransigent, existential inundation.

And when they thunder up their storm of metal hooves
On roads stamped flat by weight of blasphemy and hubris,
You testify by the crunch of oats and quiet breezes
To he who sleeps with the horizon at his foot.

To he who wakens birds with nightmare clamoring,
Who lovingly will urge the earthy spring to spread,
And flees, the charming coward, through the gloom of trees
Your disk of glowing grace above his crazy head.

Other Poems
1911-1943

THE CHILD BEFORE THE TOY STORE

As I watch you, child, before the storefront window,
When you gaze upon the dreams that can't be had,
Before your eyes will rise your father's bloody trouble
And your ill mother—needle always in her hand.

I see an attic chamber or a darkened basement,
A stuffy stench where wicked Poverty has foraged,
And there a mother weeping in her sad-eyed silence,
And a weary father with his furrowed forehead.

As I watch you, child, you look so rapturously
At everything that seems to you a fairy story—
What's near and out of reach is like a golden calling,

O! Then I feel within your heart each little tremor:
The joyfulness that windowpane will ever temper,
The wish gone unfulfilled that's universal longing.

1911

REQUEST

Let there be some warriors,
Let them dress in armor,
Let them have swords and bucklers...
...Let others be like flowers...

Let there be some for action,
Let temples twist with laurels,
...Others—blooming with jasmine,
Let others quietly grumble...

Let some fight! And let them
With mighty hands crush misfortune!
...Let others in fields at gloaming
Go humming songs of longing...

Let these and those be taken
As Spiritual oblations,
Although some will be warriors,
And others be like flowers.

1912

POEM

About what? About some evening.
With wine and June's warm halo.
Stars, like flowers, happily
Fleeing through heavenly meadows.

Riding along the Passage
How the horse was elated,
How the moon above us
The jagged cloud indented.

Not that anything happened,
Not a thing was mentioned.
Anyway I was alone then,
You weren't even present.

1923

WARSAW

What a wonderment is Warsaw!
All the houses, all the people!
All the pride and all the pleasure
In our hearts the city kindles!

All the streets, the schools, the gardens,
Plazas, shopping, hustle, traffic,
Cinemas and transportation
And the promenades and districts!

Ancient Vistula delighting
In the capital grown shapely,
Thinking back when she was tiny,
And today she's such a lady.

1935

THE HARVEST

to my sister Irena

Using grains instead of flowers let us sow
Our fathers' graves. That when the earth mill minces them,
They will ascend, the dead, in stalky presences
Demanding a resounding harvesting of woe.

So then—go to the cemeteries, daughters and sons,
Forage the tombstone pasture for the earthly remnants.
And shuck the ears of grain, and eat them like a sacrament—
Instruct the young that this grave: it is a living one.

1937

FATHER

I once had thought that I was able
To give eternity through prayers,
That they'd somehow smooth your passage,
So you might find eternal solace.
Today—all that a son can manage,
Is just to look, to sigh—meander
Towards the wall to fix your photo,
When it hangs crooked.

1943

Original Polish Titles

Czyhanie na Boga (1918)

Teofania	3
Dusza	4
Ogień	5
Szczęście	6
Malarz	7
Przymierze	8
Pieśń o radości i rytmie	9
Spadek	10
Pan	11
Helios	12
Chrystus	13
Solenizanci	14
Chrystus miasta	15
Staruszkowie	17
Ogrody szpitalne	18
Symfonia wieków	19
Atak	20
Jak wiersz powstaje	21
Brzoskwinia	22
Zdrada	23
Lilia	24

Sokrates tańczący (1920)

    Nasza mądrość   27

    Vanitas   28

    Dialog   29

    Zmęczony burz szaleństwem…   30

    Litania   31

    Mróz nędzarzy   33

    Sokrates tańczący   35

    Dwa wiatry   39

    Życie moje   40

Siódma jesień (1922)

    Imię   43

    Zły wiersz   44

    Ojczyzna   45

Wierszy tom czwarty (1923)

    Śmierć   49

    My—ludzie   50

    Nauka   51

    Rachunek   53

    W lesie   55

    Rzeź brzóz   56

Słowa we krwi (1926)

Słowo i ciało	59
Sitowie	64
Słowem do krwi!	65
Buty	66
Mieszkanie	67
Cocktail	68
Sprawozdanie z podróży na Wystawę...	69
Spacer fantastyczny w lesie Fontainebleau	70
Wtedy	71
Nieznane drzewo	72

Rzecz Czarnoleska (1929)

Źródło	77
Matematyka	78
Bagdad, *czyli o przyszłym poecie*	79
Melodia	80
O moim stole	81
Słówko o księżycu w stawie	82
Sufit	83

Biblia cygańska (1933)

Biblia cygańska	87

Trawa	88
Suma jesieni	89
Muza	90
Trudy majowe	91
Do prostego człowieka	92

Treść gorejąca (1936)

Czterdzieści wiosen	97
Zadymka	98
To było tak...	99
Daleki tygrys	101
Przedwiośnie	103
Puste mieszkanie	104
***Z okruszynami młodości - co robić?	105
Erratum	106
Do Boga	107

Inne wiersze (1911-1943)

Dziecko przed sklepem z zabawkami	111
Prośba	112
Wiersz	113
Warszawa	114
Żniwo	115
Ojciec	116